Caribbean Canvas

For Mark and our new little one,
who stayed in me belly
till this was done...

Frané Lessac
Caribbean Canvas

Staff Boat (Palm Island), Oil on Canvas Board, 30 x 25 inches

J. B. Lippincott  New York

The Song of the Banana Man

Up in de hills, where the streams are cool,
Where mullet an' janga swim in de pool,
I have ten acres of mountain side,
An' a dainty-foot donkey dat I ride,
Four Gros Michel, an' four Lacatan,
Some coconut trees, and some hills of yam,
An' I pasture on dat very same lan'
Five she-goats an' a big black ram.

Evan Jones

The Song of the Banana Man

Down at de bar near United Wharf
We knock back a white rum, bus' a laugh,
Fill de empty bag for further toil
Wid saltfish, breadfruit, coconut oil.

Evan Jones

Rum Bar (Barbados), Oil on Canvas Board, 30 x 25 inches

"You live in de cement house, and no worry de hurricane."

West Indian proverb

"Pumpkin neba bear water-melan."
Children resemble parents.

West Indian proverb

Day Care Centre (Nevis), Oil on Canvas Board, 30 x 20 inches

South

But today I recapture the islands'
bright beaches blue mist from the ocean
rolling into fishermen's houses.
By these shores I was born: sound of the sea
came in at my window, life heaved and breathed
in me then with the strength of that
turbulent soil.

Edward Brathwaite

Island Fishing (Redonda), Mixed Media Collage, 10 x 8 inches

Sea School

So for an hour, an age, I swam with them,
One with a peace that might go on forever...
Till, of a sudden, quick as a falling net,
Some thought embraced them. I watched them go
Tidily over the reef, where I could not follow.

Barbara Howes

Undersea (Tobago Cays), Oil on Canvas, 40 x 36 inches

Jamaican Alphabet

A fe ackee, salt fish bes' frien, an'
B fe bammy, banana an' den
C fe coco an' callalloo, an'
D is fe dumplin an' duckanoo, duckanoo.

Louise Bennett

Schoolboys (Grenada), Oil on Canvas Board, 25 x 30 inches

"Break master neck but nuh break master law."
Respect the law.

West Indian proverb

Officer Troutman (Barbados), Oil on Canvas Board, 25 x 30 inches

Market Women

Down from the hills, they come
With swinging hips and steady stride
To feed the hungry town.
They stirred the steep dark land
To place within the growing seed.
And in the rain and sunshine
Tended the young green plants,
They bred, and dug and reaped.
And now, as Heaven has blessed their toil,
They come, bearing the fruits,
These hand-maids of the soil.
Who bring baskets down,
To feed the hungry town.

Daisy Myrie

Vegetable Market (St. Kitts), Oil on Canvas Board, 25 x 30 inches

Ilan' Life

Ilan' life ain' no fun less ya treat errybody
Like ya brudder, ya sister, or ya frien'
Love ya neighbor, play ya part, jes remember
das de art
For when ocean fence ya in, all is kin.

Susan J. Wallace

Boys Fishing (Antigua), Oil on Canvas Board, 26 x 18 inches

An old Jamaican woman thinks about the hereafter

What would I do forever in a big place, who
have lived all my life in a small island?
The same parish holds the cottage I was born in, all
my family, and the cool churchyard.

A. L. Hendricks

Pink Church (Antigua), Oil on Canvas Board, 20 x 24 inches

The Hymn Tunes

I sang off-key on Low Church, tropical
Sunday mornings; organ swept, never doubted
That the sure tunes had reason to be sure,
That some great good would come of what I shouted.
Later, across the sea, I sang in a tall
Gothic cathedral, where all sounds endure.

Edward Lucie-Smith

Salem Church (Montserrat), Watercolor on Paper, 16 x 12 inches

This time, from across the water
I found Blondella gone.
Beautiful brown Blondella
who between selling rum and rotis
sipped at her favorite gin and tonic
staggering slightly in the sun.
But now gone.
(Some say) Miami. Antigua.
Across the water (somewhere).

C. Aleph Kamal

Cargo Boat (Mayreau), Oil on Canvas Board, 30 x 25 inches

Kinky Hair Blues

Lord 'tis you did gie me
All dis kinky hair.
'Tis you did give me
All dis kinky hair,
And I don't envy gals
What got dose locks so fair.

Una Marson

Disco (St. Kitts), Oil on Canvas Board, 30 x 16 inches

"Caliban" Limbo

limbo
limbo like me

drum stick knock
and the darkness is over me

knees spread wide
and the water is hiding me

limbo
limbo like me

knees spread wide
and the dark ground is under me

down

down

down

and the drummer is calling me.

Edward Brathwaite

Limbo (Barbados), Oil on Canvas Board, 30 x 22 inches

Diamonds, Hearts, Kings and Aces
Cards and Coins and familiar faces
The old wooden table
Has seen smiles and tears
of gamblers' fortunes
throughout the years.

Marcus Wayne

Cardsharks (Grenada), Oil on Canvas Board, 30 x 22 inches

An old Jamaican woman thinks about the hereafter

I have looked
up at the stars from my front verandah and have been afraid
of their pathless distances. I have never flown
in the loud aircraft nor have I seen palaces,
so I would prefer not to be taken up high nor
rewarded with a large mansion.

A. L. Hendricks

Claudia (Union Island), Oil on Canvas, 36 x 40 inches

Government House (Montserrat), Gouache on Paper, 15 x 11 inches

Acknowledgments

PAINTINGS

For permission to publish or reproduce the paintings in this book, grateful acknowledgment is made to the following: "Island Fishing": Mr. Aleph Kamal; "Disco": Ms. Jane Parfet; "Yellow House on Wall Street" and "Mr. T's Barber Shop": Mr. Chris Thomas; "Salem Church": Fowler-Mills Gallery; "Government House": Mr. and Mrs. J. Astley

POETRY

The author and publishers wish to thank the following, who have kindly given permission for the use of copyright material: Aleph Kamal for his poem "The Village Place." Oxford University Press for "Caliban" from *Islands* by Edward Kamau Brathwaite (1969), and with Doubleday & Company Inc. for an extract from "South" by Edward Kamau Brathwaite. Douglas Rae (Management) Ltd. on behalf of Evan Jones for an extract from "The Song of the Banana Man." Edward Lucie-Smith for an extract from "The Hymn Tunes." Marcus Wayne for his poems "The Old Wooden Table" and "Schooldays." Every effort has been made to trace all the copyright holders, but if any have been inadvertently overlooked, the publishers will be pleased to make the necessary arrangement at the first opportunity.

Caribbean Canvas
Copyright © 1987 by Frané Lessac
First published by Macmillan Publishers Ltd, London and Basingstoke
Printed in the U.S.A. All rights reserved.
Typography by Andrew Rhodes
1 2 3 4 5 6 7 8 9 10
First American Edition, 1989

Library of Congress Cataloging-in-Publication Data
Lessac, Frané.
    Caribbean canvas / Frané Lessac.
      p.   cm.
    Summary: The artwork of Frané Lessac accompanies this collection
of poems by various Caribbean poets, including Robert Johnson,
Edward Brathwaite, A.L. Hendricks, Evan Jones, and others.
      ISBN 0-397-32367-0 : $. — ISBN 0-397-32368-9 (lib. bdg.) :
$
    1. Lessac, Frané—Themes, motives.   2. Antilles, Lesser, in art.
3. Children's poetry. [1. Caribbean Area in art.   2. Caribbean
poetry (English)—Collections.]   1. Title.
ND315.L47L42 1989   88-36555
759.13—dc19   CIP
                                                   AC